120 Social Media Profile Tips

Cesar Pietri

Introduction

This ebook will give you 120 social media profile concepts. You'll have all kinds of ideas for different information to add to your social networking web page profiles. The more personal and professional information you give your prospects the more likely they will become your friend or followers and purchase your products. This kind of information can boost you credibility, authority, expertise and create rapport and trust with your leads.

1) You could add your age and your mental characteristics to your web site profile. Many people add their best habits and total net worth. A final point is you can add your favorite luxury car and yard game.

2) You may advertise the awards you won and your heritage in your social profile. Plenty of people advertise airports they traveled on and their biggest pet peeve. To close you might add your favorite lifestyle and word game.

3) You can air your best childhood memory and you physical characteristics to your forum profile. Various people list antiques they owned and the no. of years they worked as an employee. A last point is you should add your favorite leg exercises and words.

4) You might list the best choices you've made and workouts you've done to your member profile. Tons of people announce the appliances they owned and the years they've owned their business. In ending you could add your favorite law and winter sport.

5) You could announce your best college memory and wishes that came true to your follower profile. Some people author the bad habits they quit and their yearly career income. A end point is you can add your favorite language and wild animals.

6) You may author your best family vacation and about your neighbors to your chat profile. A number of people bring up beaches they've visited and the year they retired. To end you might add your favorite landmark and web site.

7) You can bring up your best friends and where your meant spouse to your networking profile. Certain people broadcast the best compliment they've got and their work stories. And finally you should add your favorite kid game and weather.

8) You might broadcast your best friends in college and what web site you often visit to your friend profile. Several people catalog boats they've owned and their work goals they've completed. In closing you could add your favorite joke and water sport.

9) You could catalog your best friends in school and weird things you've done to your blog profile. Numerous people add buildings they own and what music they listen too. And lastly you can add your favorite jewelry and visuals.

10) You may list your best memory as a children and the weight you've lost to your subscriber profile. Many people chronicle cabins they own and what movies they've watched. To finalize you might add your favorite investment and video game to it.

11) You can chronicle your best memory of your friends and your current weight to your messaging profile. Plenty of people comment on canyons they've visited and what magazines they often read. And to end you should add your favorite invention and vehicle.

12) You might circulate your best memory of your grandparents and weekend activities to your fan profile. Various people communicate cars they own and ways they've made money fast. In conclusion you could add your favorite indoor sport and vegetable.

13) You could comment on your best memory of your parents and your normal weekday activities to your web site profile. Tons of people compose celebrity parties they've attended and types of outsourcers they hire. And to conclude you can add your favorite indoor hobby and vacation activity.

14) You may communicate your best memory of your pets and wedding descriptions to your social profile. Some people convey cites they've lived in and the types of offline products they sell. To conclude you might add your favorite individual sport and vacation.

15) You can compile your best memory of your spouse and volunteer work you do to your forum profile. A number of people add the expensive clothes they own and trademarks they owned. A final statement is you should add your favorite ice cream and typical day.

16) You might compose your best physical features and vegetables you ate to your member profile. Certain people demonstrate clubs they've went to and things invested they've in. In summary you could add your favorite hotel and type of music.

17) You could construct your best vacation as a kid and values/moral ethics you have to your follower profile. Several people depict computers they've owned and subjects they've self studied. A last statement is you can add your favorite hot drink and type of movie.

18) You may convey your big tests passed and types of pets owned to your chat profile. Numerous people describe concerts they've attended and their savings account size. To close you might add your favorite home and tv shows.

19) You can craft your birth place and things you taught children to your networking profile. Many people disclose countries they've lived in and their salary amount. A end statement is you should add your favorite holiday and tv.

20) You might demonstrate your birthmarks and things you fixed to your friend profile. Plenty of people discuss countries they've visited and their resumes/applications. In sum you could add your favorite hobby and tricks.

21) You could depict your body fat percent and things you collected to your blog profile. Various people dispatch cruises they've taken and their religion. As a final point is you can add your favorite hip hop music and training.

22) You may describe your body tone and things you cherished to your subscriber profile. Tons of people display their current location and raises they've got. To finish up you might add your favorite healthy food and toy.

23) You can disclose your books you've read and things you are proud of to your messaging profile. Some people divulge dances they've went to and promotions they've got. As a last point is you should add your favorite gift and tool.

24) You might discuss your calories a day and tattoos to your fan profile. A number of people describe their relationship with their boss and promotional tactics they've used. To recap you could add your favorite games show and tip.

25) You could dispatch your characteristics of family members and step parents names to your web site profile. Certain people draft their relationships with coworkers and promises/secrets they've kept. As a end point is you can add your favorite game and therapy.

26) You may display your children characteristics and star sign to your social profile. Several people email their relationships with friends and their professional partnerships. Lastly you might add your favorite furniture and team sport.

27) You can distribute your children names and spouse occupation to your forum profile. Numerous people describe their relationship with their grandparents and product reviews they given or received. To sum you should add your favorite fruit and taste.

28) You might divulge your children occupations and spouse name to your member profile. Many people exhibit their relationship with rest of their family and problems they've solved. Finally you could add your favorite forum and talent.

29) You could docket your Chinese sign and spouse characteristic to your follower profile. Plenty of people explain their relationship with their spouse and positive thoughts they've used. In the end you can add your favorite food and take-out food.

30) You may draft your clothes sizes and sports you play to your chat profile. Various people expose themselves as a son/daughter and positive visuals they used. To highlight you might add your favorite flower and table top game.

31) You can email your collage and sports played in school to your networking profile. Tons of people describe themselves as coworker/employee and positive visuals they use. To recall you should add your favorite speaker and SUV.

32) You might establish your collections completed and spiritual beliefs to your friend profile. Some people describe themselves as a grand parent and their positive role models. To summarize you could add your favorite fiction book and subject/topic.

33) You could exhibit your college classes taken and social networks belong too to your blog profile. A number of people describe themselves as parent and positive changes they've made. To wrap up you can add your favorite feel materials and strategy.

34) You may explain your colleges went to and social goals completed to your subscriber profile. Certain people highlight dreams they've lived and politicians they've meant or made friends with. In summarization you might add your favorite fast food and stories.

35) You can expose your cosmetic procedures and snacks you've cut down on to your messaging profile. Several people identify the electronics they owned and physical obstacles they've overcome. To outline you should add your favorite fashion and stomach exercise.

36) You might express your date of birth and smartest person you've meant to your fan profile. Numerous people illustrate experiences that made them confident and phobias they've overcome. Last but not least you could add your favorite fantasy sport and stereo.

37) You could fashion your degrees earned and skin tone to your web site profile. Many people index experiences that made them laugh and fears they've overcome. Also remember you can add your favorite ezine and sports car.

38) You may file your describe personality and singer/musicians meant/friends with to your social profile. Plenty of people insert their family stories and personal obstacles overcome. My conclusion is you might add your favorite exercise equipment and sport to watch.

39) You can forge your donations you made and siblings/steps names to your forum profile. Various people introduce family/friends they've visited and people that have interviewed them. To sum up you should add your favorite exercise and sound.

40) You might form your elementary school and siblings occupations to your member profile. Tons of people issue forests they've visited and patents they own. In final analysis you could add your favorite events and soup.

41) You could formulate your extra activities in school and sibling characteristics to your follower profile. Some people jot down furniture they own and their outside activities. Last of all you can add your favorite errand and sport.

42) You may forward your extra-curricular activities in college and short term goals completed to your chat profile. A number of people key in golf courses they've played on and online businesses they've owned. One final issue is you might add your favorite environment and song.

43) You can highlight your eye color and sex to your networking profile. Certain people leak the high end animals they've owned and obsessions they've stopped. My last point is you should add your favorite electronic and software.

44) You might identify your eye sight and school awards to your friend profile. Several people list historical places they visited and number of testimonials they've gotten. One can conclude you could add your favorite ebook and social network.

45) You could illustrate your famous autographs got and scholarships/grants earned to your blog profile. Numerous people log in home decorations they've bought and their number of paid members. A final point is you can add your favorite DVD and snack.

46) You may index your favorite college profession and sacrifices you made for someone to your subscriber profile. Many people write the home services they've bought and number of outsourcers they use. To close you might add your favorite drawing and smells.

47) You can insert your favorite game and romantic things you've done to your messaging profile. Plenty of people record their home town and the number of friends/followers they have. A last point is you should add your favorite dog and skill.

48) You might introduce your favorite playground equipment and romantic things done to you to your fan profile. Various people mention how their employees would describe them and number of franchises they own. In ending you could add your favorite doctor and singer.

49) You could invest in your favorite school subjects and professional obstacles overcame to your web site profile. Tons of people note how they celebrated birthdays and their number of employees. A end point is you can add your favorite dinosaur and shoes.

50) You may issue your favorite subjects and professional help you had to your social profile. Some people offer how they maintained their weight and the number of bestselling products they have. To end you might add your favorite diet food and seminars.

51) You can jot down your favorite teacher and prizes won to your forum profile. A number of people paste how they manage pain and their number of back links. And finally you should add your favorite diamond and self help ebook.

52) You might key in your first name and prayers that were answered to your member profile. Certain people pencil in how they persuade people and the niches/markets they are in. In closing you could add your favorite desert and secrets learned.

53) You could launch your fears you overcome and political views to your follower profile. Several people point out how they relaxed and the newspapers they are mentioned in. And lastly you can add your favorite affiliate contests won and season.

54) You may leak your fears you've overcome and piercings to your chat profile. Numerous people post how they saved the environment and they natural disasters they overcome. To finalize you might add your favorite decade and sculptures.

55) You can list your financial disasters you survive and pet names to your networking profile. Many people present how they sleep well and the most successful product they've launch. And to end you should add your favorite date and school.

56) You might log your financial phobias you overcome and personal things been elected for to your friend profile. Plenty of people promote how they solved problems and the most annoying things to them. In conclusion you could add your favorite dances and scary movie.

57) You could manifest your first spouse date and personal goals completed to your blog profile. Various people provide how they stayed motivated and their monthly income. And to conclude you can add your favorite dance and sandwich.

58) You may manufacture your first spouse kiss and people you've help to your subscriber profile. Tons of people publicize how they stayed organized and money you've won. To conclude you might add your favorite culture and salad.

59) You can market your friend characteristics and people you trust to your messaging profile. Some people publish how they stay sanitary and their memorable advice. A final statement is you should add your favorite craft and romantic date.

60) You might mention your friend names and people you respect to your fan profile. A number of people put cross how they stayed self confident and their media mentions. In summary you could add your favorite course and rock music.

61) You could note your friend occupations and parents/step names to your web site profile. Certain people put together how they've stopped negative emotions and their media appearances. A last statement is you can add your favorite country music and restaurant.

62) You may offer your funniest person you meant and parents occupations to your social profile. Several people put up how they stopped negative thoughts and the marketing techniques they used. To close you might add your favorite country and resource.

63) You can organize your gifts you bought kids and parents characteristics to your forum profile. Numerous people recite the jewelry they've owned and major skills they've learned. A end statement is you should add your favorite contact sport and report.

64) You might paste your gifts you've given and paranormal beliefs to your member profile. Many people recommend the lakes they've visited and magazines they've been published in. In sum you could add your favorite computer game and relaxation activity.

65) You could pencil in your gifts you've received and motivational music listen too to your follower profile. Plenty of people record the landmarks they've visited and magazine they've had covers on. As a final point is you can add your favorite computer and recreation.

66) You may pitch your good habits you started and models meant/friends with to your chat profile. Various people owners reference the limos they've traveled in and loans they've got. To finish up you might add your favorite commercial and recipe.

67) You can point out your grades you got in college and mistakes/errors you learned from to your networking profile. Tons of people register the motorcycles they've owned and the kinds of employees they hire. As a last point you should add your favorite comedy show and quote.

68) You might post your grades you got in school and miracles that happen to you to your friend profile. Some people release the mountains they've visited and the kind of outsourcers they use. To recap you could add your favorite color and public speaker.

69) You could prepare your grand children characteristics and miracles that happen to your blog profile. A number of people relinquish the museums they've visited and the jobs they've had. As a end point you can add your favorite college and politician.

70) You may present your grand children names and mental obstacles overcome to your subscriber profile. Certain people remark on the neighbors they've had and their job responsibilities. Lastly you might add your favorite cold drink and podcast.

71) You can promote your grand children occupations and mental business problems overcome to your messaging profile. Several people render their normal bed time and their investment income. To sum you should add your favorite coffee and plant.

72) You might provide your hair color and memorable tips to your fan profile. Numerous people report their normal wake up time and their income from selling business. Finally you could add your favorite coach and pizza.

73) You could publicize your hair length and memorable stories to your web site profile. Many people reveal the number of products they sell and how they mentally attract money. In the end you can add your favorite club and picture.

74) You may publish your hair style and memorable quotes to your social profile. Plenty of people roll out their number of services and how they've helped the environment. To highlight you might add your favorite clothes and pick-up line.

75) You can push your health goals completed and memorable conversations to your forum profile. Various people say the off road vehicles owned and how their children would describe them. To recall you should add your favorite city and phrase/saying.

76) You might put cross your health problems you've overcome and limiting beliefs overcame to your member profile. Tons of people record their opt-in list size and hours a week they work. To summarize you could add your favorite chore and photo.

77) You could put together your height and insults you took constructively to your follower profile. Some people say outrageous things they've done and days they work a week. To wrap up you can add your favorite chat rooms and pet.

78) You may put up your heroic feats and inside activities to your chat profile. A number of people share the people in their mastermind group and hobbies they have. In summarization you might add your favorite cell phone and painting.

79) You can recite your high school and injures you overcome to your networking profile. Certain people show people that quoted you and their happy stories. To outline you should add your favorite CD and outside hobby.

80) You might recommend your how improve memory and improvements you've make to your friend profile. Several people sound about personal talents they learned and their favorite business quotes. Last but not least you could add your favorite cat and outfit.

81) You could record your how improved grades and illnesses you overcome to your blog profile. Numerous people spawned phones they own and famous people they've worked for. My conclusion is you can add your favorite casino and online videos.

82) You may reference your how long been married and how you've help people to your subscriber profile. Many people speak pools/hot tube they owned and famous endorsements they've got. To sum up you might add your favorite career and online hobby.

83) You can register your how many books own and how you thought positive to your messaging profile. Plenty of people speak about products they've offer and their famous customers. In final analysis you should add your favorite card game and online audio.

84) You might release your how many people you dated and how you saved time to your fan profile. Various people specify products they've invented and experts they've learned from. Last of all you could add your favorite car and Olympic sport.

85) You could relinquish your how many times married and how you celebrated reunions to your web site profile. Tons of people state radio shows they've been mentioned on and etiquette they've learned. One final issue is you can add your favorite candy bar and off rood vehicle.

86) You may remark your how many times you fell in love and how you celebrated holidays to your social profile. Some people state radio shows they've been mentioned on and drinks they've drank. My last point is you might add your favorite candy and number.

87) You can render your how much you can lift and how would spouse describe you to your forum profile. A number of people submit their ranks in search engines and describe their self as boss. One can conclude you should add your favorite camping trip and non-fiction book.

88) You might report your how prevented health problems and how would parents describe you to your member profile. Certain people suggest their reoccurring income streams and describe their self as a friend. A final point is you could add your favorite business and newspaper.

89) You could reveal your how you avoided negative people and how would grandparents describe you to your follower profile. Several people supply the reseller books they wrote and describe their relationship with their parents. To close you can add your favorite breakfast food and newsletter.

90) You may roll out your how you became a leader and how would co workers describe you to your chat profile. Numerous people support restaurants they ate at and describe their relationship with employees. A last point is you might add your favorite book and news story.

91) You can say your how you dealt with difficult people and how would boss describe you to your networking profile. Many people talk about seas they've visited and the debts paid off. In ending you should add your favorite boat and news show.

92) You might script your how you eliminated distractions and healthy foods ate to your friend profile. Plenty of people state the seminars they've attended and their current job/career. A end point is you could add your favorite board games and nature area.

93) You could send your how you eliminated stress and happiest person you meant to your blog profile. Various people transmit the services they offer and their current business. To end you can add your favorite blog and musician.

94) You may set up your how you gained positive emotions and funny stories to your subscriber profile. Tons of people twitter the size of their business building and their credit score. A final point is you can add your favorite biography and music instrument.

95) You can share your how you improved senses and fruits you ate to your messaging profile. Some people type the size of their homes and the credit cards they owned. To close you might add your favorite bands and music.

96) You might show your how you lost weight and friendship goals completed to your fan profile. A number of people uncover skyscrapers they been in and their credit card limits. A last point is you should add your favorite audio book and muscle car.

97) You could sound out your how you made family time and friendliness person you meant to your web site profile. Certain people unveil social networks their on and copyrights they owned. In ending you could add your favorite athletic team and movie.

98) You may spawned your junior high school and famous people meant to your social profile. Several people upload software they've created and contests they've won. A end point is you can add your favorite athlete and mountain.

99) You can speak your last name and famous athletes meant/friends with to your forum profile. Numerous people voice something they invented and their consulting/coaching fee. To end you might add your favorite artist and model.

100) You might speak out your lefty/righty and family goals completed to your member profile. Many people write sports stuff they owned and coaches/consultant they've hired. And finally you should add your favorite article and micro blog.

101) You could specify your long term goals completed and failures overcome to your follower profile. Plenty of people add states they've lived in and classes they've taught. A final point is you can add your favorite art work and mentor.

102) You may start your major things you've learned and experts/gurus meant/friends with to your chat profile. Various people advertise states they've visited and charities they've donated too. To close you might add your favorite arm exercise and membership/club.

103) You can state your make up used and experts you've meant/hired to your networking profile. Tons of people allot the hours a week they work and business they've sold. A last point is you should add your favorite appliance and meat.

104) You might submit your marriage proposal description and experiences that made you happy to your friend profile. Some people announce theater shows they've attended and the business titles owned. In ending you could add your favorite antiques and meal.

105) You could suggest your meats you've ate and disability you got over to your blog profile. A number of people author things they are famous for and their business stories. A end point is you can add your favorite alcohol drink and magazine.

106) You may supply your medical history and dessert you cut down on to your subscriber profile. Certain people bring up things they've been elected for and their business responsibilities. To end you might add your favorite actress and radio station.

107) You can support your middle name and dares done to your messaging profile. Several people broadcast their times shares owned and business people they've modeled. And finally you should add your favorite actor and tire.

108) You might syndicate your names of other family members and compulsions you had to your fan profile. Numerous people catalog tours they've taken and their business milestones. In closing you could add your favorite gum and baseball team.

109) You could talk about your number of children and common family activities to your web site profile. Many people chat about tv shows mentioned on and business licenses they have. And lastly you can add your favorite truck and dressing.

110) You may tell your number of friends and church belong to to your social profile. Plenty of people chronicle tv's owned and books you've wrote. To finalize you might add your favorite job and cup.

111) You can throw together your number of grand children and chores you enjoy to your forum profile. Various people comment type of offline services and your biggest sale. And to end you should add your favorite chair and reality show.

112) You might transmit your number of parents and business obstacles overcome to your member profile. Tons of people communicate type of online services and your biggest raise. In conclusion you could add your favorite role-playing game and motorcycle.

113) You could twitter your number of pets and body language you use to your follower profile. Some people compose types of digital products and biggest promotion. And to conclude you can add your favorite texture and hockey team.

114) You may type your other family members and best decisions you made to your chat profile. A number of people convey types of employees you have and your biggest check. To conclude you might add your favorite day and carpet.

115) You can uncover your preschool and bad habits you've ended to your networking profile. Certain people record their unusual talents and the best legal advice they got. A final statement is you should add your favorite feel and album.

116) You might unveil your relationship goals completed and bad habits you quit to your friend profile. Several people demonstrate video games you played/solved and your best idea. In summary you could add your favorite football team and emotion.

117) You could upload your relationship problems you overcame and awards you won to your blog profile. Numerous people depict what books you've read and your best friends at work/business. A last statement is you can add your favorite toothpaste and bed.

118) You may vend your restaurant are at and affiliations you used to your subscriber profile. Many people describe what newspaper you often read and your best business advice. To close you might add your favorite dishes and riddle.

119) You can voice your running mile time and addictions you've stopped to your messaging profile. Plenty of people disclose what TV shows they watched and the best advice you got. A end statement is you should add your favorite month and basketball team.

120) You might whip up your self help book you bought and actors/actresses meant/friends with to your fan profile. Various people discuss zoo you visited and your average daily traffic. In summary, you could add your favorite mp3 and talk show.